RICHARD DANIR

SPIRITS IN THE WELL

FOR SOPRANO AND PIANO

AMP 8212

First Printing: May 2012

ISBN: 978-1-4234-0868-0

Associated Music Publishers, Inc.

DISTRIBUTED BY
HAL•LEONARD®
CORPORATION
7777 W. BLUEMOUND RD. P.O. BOX 13819 MILWAUKEE, WI 53213

Spirits in the Well was composed at Yaddo in Saratoga Springs in the last weeks of November, 1997. The text to the four songs by Toni Morrison were sent by Ms. Morrison following my desire to compose a second song cycle for Jessye Norman—*Sweet Talk* (the first cycle) was composed in 1996, and premiered at Carnegie Hall, New York in April 1997. What emerged was a darker, less florid and perhaps more intimate piece than *Sweet Talk*. I was also interested in writing a work for voice and piano alone, as none of my dozen or so works involving voice had been set for that very standard combination.

So, why did this piece need to be written? Simply because of my deep identification with Ms. Morrison's lyrics, and my profound appreciation for the way Ms. Norman approaches and sings my music.

Spirits in the Well was commissioned by Lincoln Center for the Performing Arts, Inc. with generous support from the A.B. and Flavia McEachern Foundation. In particular I want to thank Marsha Morrison, her son, Gavin, and Jane Moss at Lincoln Center for helping to bring this work into being.

—Richard Danielpour

Spirits in the Well was premiered
by Jessye Norman, soprano, and Ken Noda, piano
on May 10, 1998 at Avery Fisher Hall,
New York, NY.

duration circa 17 minutes

I

Down in the well
Where light does not reach
Leftover smiles stir.
Some benevolence rises
From the water
Hovers at the rim.
Feel them.
The spirits in the well
Who wish you well.
Once felt, they will come again.
They will always come again.

II

At some point the world's beauty is enough.
You don't need to photograph, paint or even remember it.
It is enough.
No record needs to be kept and you don't need
Someone to share it with or tell it to.
You can let go.
The world will always be there.
While you sleep it will be there,
And when you wake.
So you can sleep now
And there is every reason to wake.

III

I envy public love.
I myself have known it only in secret
Shared it in secret
And longed, Oh longed to show it.
To say out loud what there is no need to say:
"That I have loved only you,
Surrendered my whole self reckless to you
And nobody else."
But I can't say that aloud.
I can't tell anyone
That I have been waiting for you all my life
And being chosen to wait is the reason I can.
Is the reason I can.

IV

There are no new songs
And I have sung all the songs there are.
Gold is bitter
Alabaster chill
Only loam is dark and sweet
There are no new songs
No new songs
And I have sung all the songs there are.

Texts by Toni Morrison
printed with permission

to Jessye Norman

SPIRITS IN THE WELL

Toni Morrison

I

Richard Danielpour
(1998)

Slowly, but with forward motion (con rubato)

♪ = ca. 72–76

Down _____ in the well Where _ light ____ does not

II

At some ___ point ___ the world's ___ beau-

III

Con rubato ♩ = 60–63

But I can't say that a-loud. I can't tell a-ny-one

That I have been wait - - ing for you all my life

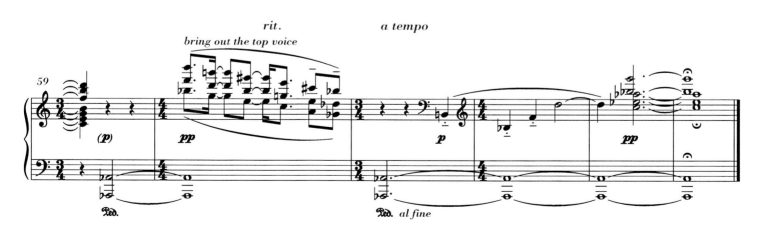